Presented to:

Butler Area Public Library

In Memory of
Donna Conklin

Donor
Neighbors on N. Duffy Road

Creativity with flowers

Bouquets

Per Benjamin
Max van de Sluis
Tomas De Bruyne

stichting
kunstboek

Egyptian bouquet

The history of the bouquet

The bouquet has followed Man's desire for creativity and love of flowers throughout the ages. I think we all can remember our first 'bouquet' – flowers picked in the countryside and put together randomly in our hands, most beautifully we thought at the time! Flowers as pure beauty and ways of expressing emotions have been part of the whole human existence. There is a lot of evidence of this from Mesopotamian and Egyptian civilizations. But even from earlier African times we know people used flowers in their lives as well. There were works of all elaborate shapes and techniques, many bouquet-like in appearance, but the bouquet as we know it today dates from the Renaissance period. The word bouquet comes from the French *bosquet* and means 'little forest'. How flowers have been, and still are, used and arranged is a result of many cultural influences. To show the etymology of the bouquet, the variations in styles, uses and techniques, we will take you all on a personal journey through history that will bring some understanding and give inspiration.

Flowers have followed mankind through the ages and reflected developments and changes in people's ways of life. In East Africa, discoveries in old burial sites from the Palaeolithic period suggest that flowers were gathered and used as a mourning tribute to the dead. A more elaborate use of flowers is first seen around 6000 BC in the Mesopotamian kingdoms between the Euphrates and the Tigris, today's Iraq, where priests and kings ruled. Fantastic palaces and temples were erected in honour of earthly and heavenly powers, all decorated with flowers. Wreaths and garlands were the norm, but also arrangements have been found that looked more like bouquets.

This first known bouquet form dated from these kingdoms but was later made famous in Egypt. Shaped like a torch, flowers were layered in circles on top of each other tied with raffia or papyrus around a papyrus stem; arranged in importance of each flower with the holiest one, the lotus, on top. The lotus was the symbol of Egypt and the life-giving Nile, the flower itself, with its yellow centre and outstretched petals, a reflection of Ra, the Sun god. Other flowers, foliage and fruits used in order of importance were: roses (Rosa), poppies (Papaver), violets (Viola), chrysanthemum, olives (Olea), celery, iris and various delphiniums, all more similar to wild flowers than today's cultivated varieties. These bouquets were used in various sizes, along with many other flower works, in religious ceremonies, funerals of pharaohs and other important people, and at official occasions as well as privately among the rich as gifts to the host of a party. Flowers were always on the list of things needed when a pharaoh was travelling with his court. These bouquets never ended up in water; they were purely for the beauty of the moment. This model of a bouquet was, up until the first part of the 20th century, sold on markets in the Middle East and Egypt.

In ancient Greece, flowers, wreaths, garlands and small simple bouquets were sold in the town squares. We could say there was a profession of flower binders;

First bouquet

Baroque bouquet

one of history's first known 'florists' was Glycera of Greece. The bouquets were often small and made of wild flowers: violets, olive blossoms and most important of all, roses. Here we see a distinction between male and female in flower use for the first time in history! Women always used lots of flowers and colours while the men mostly used only greenery in theirs. Flowers were used as symbols for gods, politicians, warriors and Olympic winners. Love, happiness and mourning were all communicated through them. To court a girl, small bouquets were left on her doorstep and newborn children were announced with small wreaths or bouquets, olives for boys and violets and roses for girls. Even life's last stage, death, was announced with cypress (Cupressus). Material and colours were very important to the Greeks as symbols in life both for people and gods.

In ancient Rome, a great metropolis with people from all over the Roman Empire, flowers were sold around the city and were an important part of life. The influences drew from Greek floral use, continuing and improving on techniques and an excess of material made possible through better growing techniques and imports from Egypt which led to an opulent and luxurious use of flowers. There were special celebrations like the *Floralia* in honour of the goddess Flora, where people gathered in the streets making wreaths and bouquets and processing to her temple to give them as offerings. Romans liked flowers for their colour and more so for their scents. They preferred flowers like violets, hyacinths, matthiola and, most importantly of all, the rose. Roses were grown on great areas and even imported from Egypt during the winter when the local supply was sparse. The rose was the symbol of love in Greek mythology and now became the flower of fashion.

Later, after the fall of the Roman Empire, when the Christian church became the new power, the opulent and excessive use of flowers, amongst other things, was banned for being symbols of old religious mythology, acclaimed being theft from God himself. The Middle Ages were also a dark time for the bouquet. But there was some light in the darkness! As a contradiction, and under the pressure of people and traditions, the church itself took many flowers as their symbols. The white rose symbolised the Virgin Mary and the red rose stood for Christ. What was spoken under the rose – *sub rosa* – was said in confidence, during confession. The rose, once the most popular flower in Rome, now became a symbol of the Christian religion! Flowers were grown and arranged in the monasteries and used both for medical use and pure beauty. From tapestries of the time we also know that flowers and vase arrangements were used at the royal courts around Europe.

The Renaissance brought the rebirth of floral design and the arts in general. The focus changed from religion towards secularised science, also for the use of flowers. Their use is widely spread from the monasteries to ordinary people via the royal courts. Flowers were formed into wreaths and garlands; petals used for beauty and perfume on tables and more. This is also when we actually started putting flowers in vases. The vase was a fact. The word itself comes from the French *vase*, Latin *vas* meaning 'container'. Slowly over the time the bouquet now replaced wreaths and garlands as the most prominent flower work. The bouquet as we know it today sees the light in this period of many changes. The Europeans discovered new continents, bringing back, among many things, new flowers. The most famous at the time was the sunflower (Helianthus). The style emphasized on a mass of flowers in bright contrasting colours, often in the fashionable system of three colours, triadic, with a conical shape with the most spectacular and valuable flowers put in the top and those of lesser importance and size at the base.

Cotillion bouquet

During the next decades there was a lot of talk about bouquets, but in reality they were more or less loosely arranged flowers in containers and vases, what we today would call arrangements. But during the late 1700s and 1800s – the Baroque and Rococo periods – when lots of new fascinating flowers such as orchids, Chinese roses, peonies (Paeonia) and tulips (Tulipa) came to Europe, botanic science became popular. We see passionate trends raging in different countries. Fritillaries, hyacinths (Hyacinthus) and, most famously of them all, tulips became not only a trend but a craze in desire and speculation. The 'tulip mania' was not unlike today's stock speculations! During the Baroque period, the 'masculine', more pompous and darker of the two, the style was rich in materials and colours, with the purpose of showing off wealth, often by using accessories like new tropical fruits, exotic birds, butterflies and all kinds of rare things.

During the Rococo, the more 'feminine', graceful and brighter of the two, the trends were once again set by the royal courts, especially the French. Hand-held bouquets became fashionable: small, round, slightly domed, tight bouquets finished off with a collar of lace or paper and, if really exclusive, in a specially designed bouquet holder of silver or some other valuable material. Flowers of a wide range were used but popular amongst many were roses, carnations (Dianthus), myrtle (Myrthus), fuchsia and citrus blooms. An even more exquisite bouquet was the one for the *décolletage* of the dress, where often a glass tube or vase was sewn in especially for the bouquet. Another bouquet for special use was the Toilet bouquet, a richly scented bouquet for the occasion of the official toilet, the dressing ceremony among the rich. Other popular bouquets were the Pompadour bouquet which was a lighter, more openly bound, bouquet also with a collar of paper or lace made with a backing, making it easy to lay it down. Other crescent-shaped bouquets like the Pompadour also became modern. Finally we have the Cotillion bouquet, after the Cotillion waltz, the 'flower waltz', where the men gave a little bouquet to their favourite lady and asked her for a dance. The lady with the most bouquets was of course the queen of the evening!

Pompadour bouquet

During the first half of the 1900s, during the Empire period and mass industrialization, flower handicraft took big steps forward. Most bigger cities

Biedermeier bouquet

in Europe have flower markets and we see the first flower shops opening. Flowers were, up until then, sold dominantly on market places. The first known flower shop was opened in Paris by a Madame Prevost. She and her two employees became famous for their bouquets that were not only for one evening. No, the new big thing was that they lasted for some 3-4 days in a vase. These were bouquets made up from individually wired flowers, mixed after one's desire, tied together with stems all the way down in the water. Before, the most common bouquet was the straw bouquet, where each flower was placed in a straw and then tied together into a bouquet, and finally the straws were covered with ribbons. This was never intended to be put in water. The next really big trend among bouquets was the Biedermeier: a round domed or a slightly cone-shaped bouquet where the flowers are arranged in circles, all with their own material and colour. This bouquet design started in Germany under the Biedermeier époque, spread over Europe and was later named after that very same époque. All materials, flowers and greenery were wired, then, starting in the centre and tying along the way while creating one circle after the other, all stems parallel or totally random. We see no radial system yet. These Biedermeier bouquets were made in all sizes and fashions.

Entering the Romantic period in the second part of the 1900s, flowers became more fashionable than ever before, leading to excessive use and variation of designs. In general, bouquets got higher, bigger and more stem was used, this being possible due to better quality and better care of the flowers. All over Europe appeared fashionable flower shops catering for the needs of the rich and successful. Flowers are in fashion! The bouquets took on more and more advanced shapes and heights, all bent and arranged in the way the florist wanted with the help of wires. We see a striving towards a more natural and long-stem expression, often with a flat background or wall and the flowers presented in a slope-like manner, like a badly arranged bouquet of today! As the name signals this is a romantic period, not only the beauty of the flowers is important but more so even, their language! Bouquets were made to express emotions that might be difficult to say upfront or simply to enhance the message. Many books were written on the subject in all countries, many times conflicting and overlapping each other! Some of the more common flowers and meanings were:

Makart bouquet

    Violets (Viola) – take me with you!
    Lily of the valley (Convallaria) – quietly I have for long adored you!
    Narcissus (Narcissus) – you are too self-complacent!
    Box (Buxus) – my faithfulness is forever!
    Nettle (Urtica) – how can you be so cruel?

One can easily imagine the complexity of these bouquets and of love!
Another very odd and interesting bouquet was the Makart bouquet, especially popular in Austria and Germany, named after the painter Hans Makart. He painted these salon bouquets of dried materials, flowers and prepared

leaves and grasses like Pampas and Phoenix, done in pyramid shapes. These became later known as dust gatherers!

At the turn of the century into the early 1900s, we see a rapid development of the profession and new flower shops opening to cater to the demand from the citizens of the growing cities. The further away from nature people got and the richer they became, the bigger the need for flowers. A wider selection with better quality was available through better growing techniques and imports from the Riviera. We see proper education for florists starting, exhibitions and competitions all to strengthen and develop the profession. The bouquet is becoming an achievable luxury to people of all classes. In general, bouquets are getting bigger and more impressive with the new possibilities as mentioned above, but not until the early 1920s did we start using the radial system and the need for wire and wired flowers then slowly decreased with the rising quality of the flowers. Techniques being used were all different solutions on tying, starting from the centre adding more and more flowers on each loop or waiting till the end and tying them all together. The first of the two gives more control and was used for all more elaborate designs. The expression *à la mode* is the Nature-inspired bouquet. A bouquet with lots of garden and 'wild' flower materials like peonies, phlox, garden roses, various grasses and foliage with an open cone shape. Another common shape was the Pyramid bouquet, more open than the latter one and in the obvious shape of a pyramid. The bouquets stay rather decorative, nature-inspired with a wide variety of flowers in the same composition or with more classic materials, often using one single flower sort, like roses or carnations with foliage. They were either more open with movement or more strictly static, most of them with an obvious backside with flowers facing forward, and did not change much until the late 1960s and early 70s when new styles came in fashion.

For most of history we have seen variations of the Decorative style, but from the 1970s we see a rapid change with the introduction of the Formal linear and Vegetative styles. Overall we can say that bouquets get more attention, inspiration and skill put into them. Formal linear, the first style to overtake the Decorative style is, as the name itself indicates, all about forms of blooms and foliage and lines of stems and branches, where the search for contrasts is crucial. Contrasts in materials, textures and, most significantly, in colours, makes this style totally different to the Decorative one. Here each single material is important, compared to the Decorative style where volume and total expression are important. The style is also inspired from Japan and its Ikebana style. This gave new challenges to florists in bouquet making. Also, more and more dyed and glittery materials were added to the designs further into the 1980s, all according to fashion in general. The Vegetative style is once again something totally different, taking its inspiration from nature, habitats, seasons and ways of growing. This makes it something far away from those Nature-inspired bouquets from

Pyramid bouquet

Nature bouquet

9

Carnation bouquet

the beginning of the century that had a more natural feel in a Decorative style. What we also see in the 1980s and 90s is the use of more and more twigs, branches and other lines of botanical and artificial kinds, leading us into the next new style, the Transparent style. This started in Germany and is best described as designs where the use of stems and lines are just as important as flower heads. These worked in an overlapping manner, creating a transparent volume, falling, cascading, rising, moving in one or several directions to become the fashionable design amongst florists.

In our time, bouquet designs have become more and more personal and individual, often with a mix of styles and with a more varied use of accessory materials giving a focus on expression instead of style. Looking back we now see how the use of flowers has changed according to historical époques and availability to a constantly wider audience. Like most trends in society, things moved slowly up until the early 20th century when things starting pacing up. There was a constant change from the late 20th century into our time now, reflecting the tempo of modern life. Styles and shapes have been reused in variations of ways and still are. But now, in floristry, as in society as a whole, we are looking for that personal expression! With knowledge and inspiration from history and with today's fantastic selection and quality of flowers and all other available materials, the challenge for the designer is to show his or her talent and imagination as well as to express the message the customer wants to convey with the bouquet. Bouquets are no longer only flowers beautifully tied together; they are means of communicating emotions.

70s bouquet

The future of the bouquet

It will be more important to make bouquets of high-level design with a personal touch. We are faced with the challenge of market change, people can buy ordinary bouquets everywhere, but do not worry about this, see it as an opportunity! We must focus on design but we need to have the knowledge of styles and techniques from the past, as well as knowledge about our materials (origin, season, growth, bloom). Customers often have an emotional reason to visit us; it is our task to translate these emotions. We have to use flowers to say what they have no words for! They might want to impress, comfort, cheer up or just make someone happy. We have to give them even more than they expect. That will be the success and pleasure for tomorrow.

Function and beauty have to unite. People see colour in a bouquet first. It is an important ingredient but also one that can change fashionably fast. We have to lead trends at all times; don't be afraid to use new combinations for inspiration. Look at flowers and see the differences in their personalities! There are many possibilities, so let flowers express themselves or use them to reflect a human personality. Use their whole potential. Let colour take hold of your creations. Try combinations you find difficult or even impossible and see the new options that open up! Use additional material to enhance your message! Combine artificial materials and botanical ones. Let your curiosity lead you.

Our profession comes from nature and that is where to find solutions. But we have to look further, in architecture, commercials, video clips, car design, art etc. and also fashion. Never copy things; use your inspiration and transform it. The future has lots of challenges in store such as the diversification in our profession and the way flowers are sold. We can buy flowers anywhere but only in a good flower shop can we buy a designed, well made bouquet. By holding on to our skills and developing our design techniques we will stand strong in the future.

Bouquets can be a barometer of time and origin. Each country will have their own style and they will be the best in their product and knowledge. They reflect the situation, wealth or spirit of that specific period. Knowledge of our product, skill, how to translate the wishes of the customer is, and is going to be, very important for us florists. That is the difference between mass bouquets and individual bouquets. We see a future where more people want 'their' bouquet. Individual bouquets that clients can see themselves in, that reflect their own being and emotion. It will be more and more important to give the correct advise with a personal touch and to use our skills to make a bouquet for every individual person.

The task of the new florist will be more than only to put flowers together. It is up to us to match the right flowers, colours and shapes to match the emotions of our customers. The language of flowers is all about communication!

Step by step

Protea with flowers

Designer
Per
Materials
Protea 'King'
Limonium 'Emille'
Bouvardia
Dianthus
Rosa 'Espéranca'
Gloriosa rothschildiana
Gomphrena globosa
Hypericum
Xerophyllum asphodeloides
Pins
19 gauge wire
Translucent plastic
Hollow pin

Design This parallel bouquet is strict but playful. It is important to show the character of the Protea, the spiralling movement of the grass and the strong colours, by minimising foliage.

Technique A parallel arrangement made in and around a main flower. Use a hollow pin to pierce the Protea. Quite an oldfashioned tool, great to use and it won't cause serious damage to the flower. Finally use pins to attach and shape the design.

Emotions Happy, colourful, almost childish, so full of life! For any occasion when we want to be more relaxed and almost jocular. Flowers can express so much!

Protea with flowers

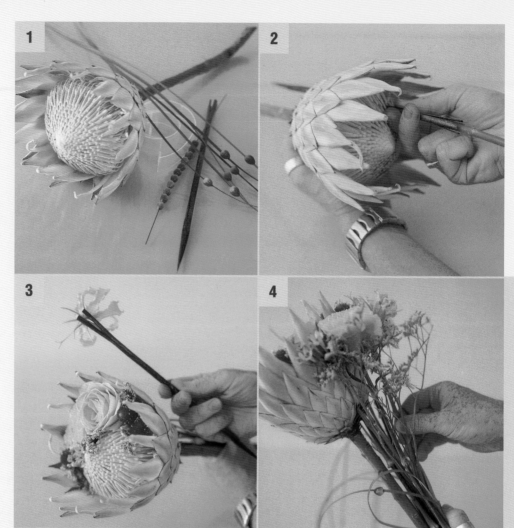

1 Choose one large Protea and strip it of all foliage to emphasise its character. Pierce Hypericums on 19 gauge wire and put them on the Bear grass stalks.

2 Then do the same with all other flowers: remove all foliage. This way, it is possible to apply the next technique. Use a big hollow pin, put a flower inside and pierce it through the Protea. Then pull the pin out so that the flower is left inside.

3 Continue in the same manner until you have filled a moon crest shape inside the Protea head. Don't cover too much of the Protea as this would ruin its character.

4 Then work on the outside of the Protea, repeating the same materials to connect both parts. Put all stems parallel to each other for a stricter expression. Finally put in the Bear grass with Hypericum before tying.

5 Now twist the Bear grass crosswise around the other stems to tighten the bouquet together. Then fix the stalk ends with pins onto the Protea.

6 Finally wrap a piece of translucent plastic in the colour of the pins around the stems. Secure it with two shorter pins.

5

6

17

Captured bouquet

Designer
Tomas
Materials
Rosa
Eustoma
Sedum
Saponaria
Corylus
Eupatorium
Panicum
Canes
Caryota branches
Daucus
Malus
Iron wire
Copper wire

Design This bouquet has a decorative shape. The power lays in the self-made top construction. The transparency lightens it all up. The flowers are tied together in a nice way. The use of apples makes it more playful.

Technique The biggest work is to bind and make the construction on top of the bouquet. The difficulty lies in the shape. Adjust the shape by weaving more canes into it but remember that the shape has to be round. The flowers are tied together in a radial way.

Emotions The construction itself takes care of the flowers from all sides. Isn't it a saying that truth and beauty come from the inside?

1 Tie a radial bouquet. Put the more delicate flowers inside the bouquet and make sure the bouquet is very compact.

2 Put small canes in between the flowers. Squeeze them in different places into the spiral. Add lots of them because they will be the base for the top construction of the bouquet. Divide them all over the bouquet.

3 Now weave the canes. They are very flexible so it is very easy to do. Place more canes on top of the construction and simply bind them together. Use thin copper wire for this. On a few places secure more canes together by adding some Caryota branches. This gives a decorative aspect to the construction.

4 Finish the construction by making it in a ball shape. Hang some apples on the wire to make the bouquet more playful.

Natural special

Designer
Max
Materials
Steel grass
Panicum 'Fountain'
Setaria italica 'Red Jewel'
Setaria italica 'Black Mountain'
Natural rough rope

Design Create a decorative bouquet of grass only using the traditional radial technique. By weaving a decorative top part over it at the end, it achieves a totally different expression, light and unexpectedly consisting of mere grasses.

Technique Start by making the radial grass bouquet, leave the Steel grass as long as possible. When the bouquet is finished you can bend the Steel grass 10 cm above the top of the bouquet and weave it irregularly, following the shape of the bouquet.

Emotions The bouquet has an outdoors picnic feeling to it but one that is special and luxurious. We used pure materials in an honest way, but with an extra touch that says: *you're special.*

23

Natural special

1 Clean the grass stalks from 20 cm from the top, to avoid leaves in the water. Be very careful not to break them.

2 For a radial arrangement, bend the stems over each other and keep twisting them in spirals. Constantly change their position in your hands to keep them under control.

3 Mix the different kinds of grass. Don't divide them equally but try to cluster them and also alternate in height. Keep the Steel grass as tall as possible, cut the bouquet at equal length and tie it with a rope.

4 Now bend the Steel grass stalks at 10 cm above the top of the bouquet and intertwine them. Follow the shape of the bouquet and create an extra transparent layer over it.

Soft pillow bouquet

Designer
Max
Materials
Rosa 'Nicole'
Dahlia 'Viking'
Paeonia lactiflora
Asclepias
Zantedeschia 'Mango'
Rosa 'Poème'
Celosia var. Cristata
Hydrangea
Cotinus coggygria
Allium sphaerocephalum
Aristolochia
1.5 mm wire
Black spool wire
Spray glue

Design This parallel decorative floral pillow is made of
Cotinus flowers on a construction of wire. We used flowers
with a soft looking texture so that everything appears
even more soft and sweet. The colours we used are
soft pink, purple, orange and red, all perfectly matching
the Cotinus.
Technique First make the construction step by step and
work very precisely. Remove the greenery from the flowers
and put them compactly in the middle. After tying put
them in a low, wide vase. With this technique you can
make many different shapes like wreaths, hearts etc.
Emotions With the Cotinus and using this technique we
created a decorative bouquet with a soft romantic feeling
that invites you to touch and feel it. The ranks make
the perfect connection with the flowers and the pillow.

Soft pillow bouquet

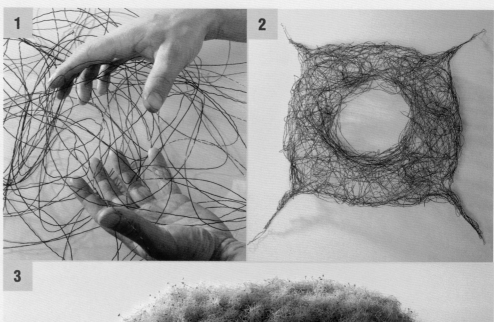

1 Unroll three reels of black wire, put everything on the floor and intertwine the wires with each other. Do not entangle them too firmly, to keep the construction open and flexible.

2 Make a hole in the middle to put the flowers in later. Shape the wire mash; keep it open but strong. From time to time, put it on the floor and look at it from a distance to check whether the shape is going the way you want. At the end make a handle with three pieces of wire. I used wire of 1.5 mm diameter.

3 Cut the Cotinus flowers off the stem and spray them with glue, then put them onto the structure. Take about ten flowers at a time, otherwise they won't stick that good. You can also use Clematis or Pampas grass instead of Cotinus.

4

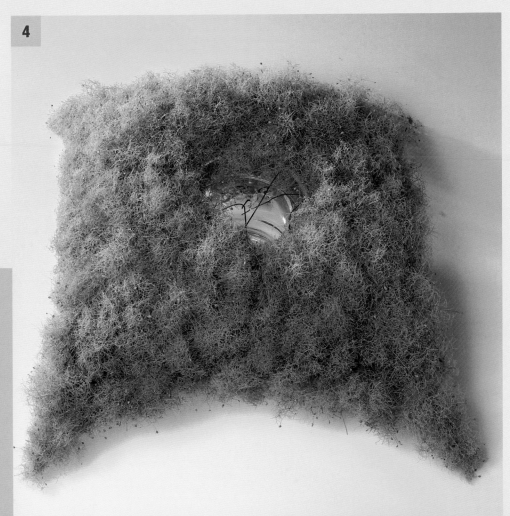

5

4 Check from a distance if the shape is right. At this stage you can still patch up little mistakes.

5 As soon as the shape is perfect, remove all the leaves of the flowers, bunch them parallel together and tuck them into the frame. Finally arrange some Aristolochia or other ranks over the finished bouquet, to make a connection between the flowers and the structure.

Nest bouquet

Designer
Tomas

Materials
Matricaria
Eustoma
Panicum
Alchemilla
Anethum
Wax flowers
Deco bind wire

Design At first sight the design looks like a bird's nest. Using lots of dead branches and a mix of springtime flowers strengthens this idea even more. Putting the flowers in a wild and random way makes the bouquet complete.
Technique The weaving method for the bird's nest together with the radial binding of the stems are the most used techniques. Weaving the flowers to hold them on the right place is of big importance here.
Emotions This nest/bouquet gives us without any doubt a springtime feeling. It is almost like looking for eggs to hatch.

1 The idea is to make a 'nest' full of flowers and evoke a springtime atmosphere. To express the right emotions, choice of colour, shape and seasonal flowers is important.

2 Start with an already made construction and add more branches to it. Make the construction as natural as possible, take a real nest as example. Add several kinds of dead branches by weaving them randomly in the construction.

3 Add flowers to the inside as well as the outside of the nest. Begin with the Wax flowers for two reasons. First they are the strongest flowers and secondly it is easy to make a first flower impression in the nest.

4 The rest of the flowers follow. Carefully use a radial technique when you bind them together. Put the flowers on different heights and do not add too many for the transparency of the bouquet.

35

Polygonum treasure wreath

Designer
Max
Materials
Alchemilla mollis
Aristolochia
Celosia var. Cristata
Polygonum
Zantedeschia 'Mango'
Rosa 'Espérance'
Rudbeckia
Setaria italica
1.5 mm wire
Black iron wire
Clear Life

Design The flowers are placed in different levels inside the Polygonum wreath. So, like a little treasure, it reveals new aspects all the time. The colours are red, orange and green, with an accent of yellow-green to bring in some lightness.
Technique Make the structure step by step and pay attention to its strength and stability. Then arrange the flowers on higher and lower layers in a parallel bouquet, to make the arrangement stronger and easier to put in a vase.
Emotions We created a strong bouquet that you can use for many different emotions, from happiness to sadness. This one has a friendly, happy summer feeling with some interesting and surprising details.

Polygonum treasure wreath

1 Weave a strong wreath of black wire. Make sure it is stable because it will be the base for the Polygonum construction. Next, fill the inside with little pieces of Polygonum, knot them tightly and secure them with cold glue. Then make a handle with thick wire – I used five pieces of 1.5 mm wire.

2 Cut the Polygonum in parts of 4 to 5 cm. Make long strings with these parts and some black spool wire. Leave an empty space of 6 to 7 cm in between each Polygonum part.

3 Twist the strings of Polygonum over and in the wreath. It is important to secure the strings regularly onto the wire construction to get a strong base. At the end spray the wreath with *Clear Life* for longevity (it won't dry out so soon).

4 Fill the wreath with flowers; avoid an equal level by mixing some taller and some shorter flowers. Then tie them in a parallel system. When it proves to be too heavy you can also tie them once in between. Lastly you make a nice connection in between the wreath and the flowers with some Aristolochia ranks.

Springtime!

Designer
Tomas
Materials
Asclepias 'Moby dick'
Matricaria
Rosa
Panicum
Anethum graveolens
Wax flowers
Canes
Typha
Rudbeckia
Yellow canes
Iron wire
Bundle wire

1 Interweave the Typha stalks with each other. The easiest technique is to put many of them onto the table in a horizontal way. Then add vertical ones one by one. Turn the ends around the edges and weave them back in: this solidifies the whole work.

2 Insert some iron wire under the woven arrangement for solidity but also for holding the construction together with the flowers. The yellow canes are added as a decorative element.

3 Cut an opening in the wired square to put the flowers through. Do this diagonally to give the bouquet a more modern and different design.

4 Now put the flowers into the woven construction. Thanks to the iron sticks you can make a radial hand-tied bouquet that holds everything together in a nice way. Let some Amaranthus flow over the construction, it will give a more natural feeling.

Design This woven and square bouquet is mainly made of Thypa. Weaving in yellow canes gives the design an extra value. By cutting the opening in a diagonal way, both ends fall nicely downwards.
Technique It is crucial to use the weaving technique as base for the bouquet. Put the flowers and the base together by sticking the iron wire into the base. Tie them all together in a radial system.
Emotions This bouquet can bring us back to springtime. It even gives us the feeling and the desire to have a picnic in the fields.

Circle of summer

Designer
Per
Materials
Dianthus
Gomphrena globosa
Xerophyllum asphodeloides
Hypericum
Lathyrus
Paeonia
Panicum
18 or 19 gauge wire
Pins

Design A very strict structured shape is combined with light decorative elements. A way of creating a modern design that still keeps that soft romantic feel. Remember not to add too much material in the centre to cover the whole we spent so much time on making!

Technique It is important to be precise and careful. Do not lift the carnations off the table before the circle is connected and the stems are made into a spiral. You will break the stems! The same goes with connecting and crossing the wires, be accurate and keep holding the flower head.

Emotions Circle of life, flowers and summer. Those pastel colours with a golden shine, all the flimsy grass-stalks blowing in the wind. An emotion of those wonderful lazy days of summer …

43

Circle of summer

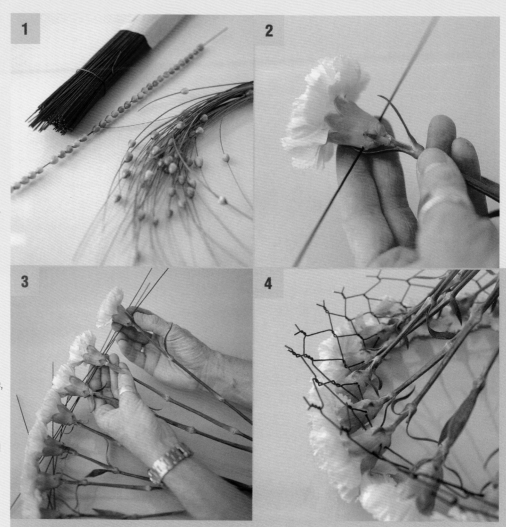

1 Pierce Hypericums on 18 gauge wire. Take off all green, otherwise it won't dry beautifully! Then place one Hypericum on each stalk of Bear grass.

2 Then take the carnations and remove all leaves except the two smaller ones under the head. Pierce each carnation with 18 or 19 gauge wire. Do this at the thicker and hardier part of the carnation head. It is also important to pierce them all on one clear horizontal line!

3 Making the circle is quite easy but takes exact and precise work. Lay one carnation on a cleared table surface, then pierce it with another one and further on. Always work from the inside out so that all wire ends stick out on the outside – imagining you are standing in the centre of the circle, of course. Stretch the long line of carnations all over the table, connect the first and the last one and order the stems into a spiral. Bundle everything together and put in a vase.

4 Now the flowers need to be secured. Place them either in a vase or upside down on a soft surface, not to damage the petals. First cross all wires between the carnation heads, work your way around. Then cross them once more, all in the way described for the 'Summer fields' bouquet (p. 89). Cut all wire ends at an equal length.

5 Weave the Bear grass into the structure, all in a criss-cross pattern and in different directions. Then attach non pierced Hypericums and Gomphrenas on each wire end for protection and decoration. Continue to add more flowers to the bouquet, untie it and place them in the usual radial manner. Make a crescent shape, mainly on the inside of the circle. Finally, to make a connection, place some Bear grass crosswise on top of the carnations and secure the stalks with pins and Gomphrenas.

Collar bouquet

Designer
Tomas
Materials
Rosa
Dahlia
Viburnum opulus
Clematis
Zinnia
Asclepias
Orchid roots
Wool
Cardboard

1 Chose several colours of wool, matching the colour range of the flowers to make the total arrangement harmonious. Cut two pieces of cardboard in round shapes and cut a hole in the middle to put the flowers in later. The cardboard will figure as a 'collar' for the bouquet.

2 Fix four sticks onto the cardboard. They will make it easier to make the bouquet and they keep the base together with the stems. Glue both pieces of cardboard onto each other to fortify the base. Use hot glue for both.

3 Tie the wool around the cardboard from the inside towards the outside. Do not concentrate on one part of the cardboard, but keep twirling the wool and redo this over and over again until the cardboard is completely covered with wool.

4 Arrange the flowers one by one in the open circles, using the radial technique. Divide them all over the arrangement. Putting berries on the cardboard will give a nice autumn feeling. Finish off by arranging the orchid roots over the bouquet.

Design This bouquet has a decorative design. The cardboard gives it more volume and a modern effect. The choice of harmonious autumnal colours finishes off the complete bouquet.
Technique Major part of the work is covering the cardboard with the wool. Once this is finished you can make a radial bouquet. By adding four sticks to the binding technique, the 'collar' stays put. You can use hot glue because it is not applied to floral materials.
Emotions This way of working with wool reminded me of my childhood. We re-used this technique and gave it a more playful, innocent feeling. It is like turning this into an impulsive design without losing control over it.

47

Plastic and petals

1

2

3

4

Designer
Per

Materials
Guzmania
Germina
Gloriosa rothschildiana
Gomphrena globosa
Dianthus
Nerine
Cattleya
18 gauge wire
Spray paint
Pins
Plastic triangles
Bullion wire

1 The basic structure for this arrangement consists of hand-made chicken wire. Make it from 18 gauge wire that you spray with copper paint to disguise it in the finished design. (Consult the 'Summer fields' bouquet on p. 89 for detailed instructions on how to make it.)

2 Place petals of Guzmania in a range of varied warm colours on the construction. Weave them in between the netting and finally secure them with orange and copper bullion wire. Work in crossing directions and reach towards the sides of the construction.

3 Hold the wire construction by its handle while arranging the flowers. Extend from the centre to the sides and make use of the spaces in between because this creates transparency and gives each flower some room. Bundle all of them in a radial system.

4 Once all flowers are placed in a mixed, playful manner and the bouquet is tied together place the plastic triangles in between where space allows you. Secure them using pins with heads in matching colours.

Design The 'traditional' dome shaped bouquet. By using an 18 gauge wire structure you can use fewer flowers while keeping a big volume. This time though cover it decoratively and disguise it as much as possible, the chicken wire is of mere technical use!

Technique A radial bouquet made inside an 18 gauge construction. The way in which the structure is made is thoroughly explained on p. 89. For placement of flowers, put their heads some centimetres away from the structure, they should not drown inside it, but give a light feeling.

Emotions A playful and almost childish bouquet for a happy, more casual moment. The colours and plastic materials play with our emotions and show the wide spectrum of what messages flowers can send.

Rich natural summer bouquet

Designer
Max
Materials
Passiflora caerulea
Rosa 'Toscanini'
Setaria italica
Rudbeckia
Campus
Asclepias
Craspedia
Zantedeschia 'Flame'
Celosia var. Cristata
Alchemilla mollis
Betula
1.5 mm iron wire

Design This bouquet is built around a structure of Betula, the major part of the design. The falling lines of the Betula and the Passiflora make it large and elegant. The reduced use of greens makes it light and graceful and prevents it from getting too massive.
Technique When you make the structure step by step, create a perfect base for a large bouquet without too many flowers. You can easily put every flower exactly where you want, on different levels so they balance. Only a radial technique is used here because this won't damage the flowers.
Emotions Our intention was to make a natural and rich looking summer bouquet with moving lines inside that link it to the table. The Betula structure makes the perfect base, the summery flowers the perfect finish.

1 Collect Betula branches that have nice hanging lines. Remove all the leaves but keep the fruit. Take a little bundle of small branches and make a circle with a diameter of ca. 12 cm. Make a handle with 1.5 mm iron wire. Don't twist the wire together otherwise it will be difficult to put in the flowers.

2 Attach the branches onto the circle. Fix them on more than one point to make it strong and steady.

3 Create different heights but keep the circle more or less open.

4 After removing most of the leaves, add the flowers, working from the outside to the middle. This bouquet is a radial design in which the branches are used to support the flowers and to create lines. Again, work with highs and lows and place the largest focal flowers in the heart of the arrangement.

55

Summer feelings

Designer
Tomas
Materials
Helianthus
Anethum
Decorative beans
Yellow canes
Iron wire
Deco bind wire

1 To create a summery mood, go for the right colours and materials. What else than yellow and sunflowers can evoke this feeling? The first thing that people see in arrangements is colour, next shape and only then material. So shape is of great importance too.

2 Make round shapes with little pieces of yellow coloured canes. Connect both ends with rough, green deco bind wire. Don't make the circles too big otherwise the playfulness will be lost. Continue until you have several of these.

3 Attach all these circles together, making a round shape. Mix the bigger with the smaller circles. Attach three canes per circle for firmness. Fix three strong sticks in the middle and attach them to each other by binding them in a radial arrangement. Those sticks will hold the flower construction on the right place.

4 Add the flowers. First put the big and dominant sunflowers all over the circle. Remember to keep the construction transparent. Then insert the Anethum flowers. Don't put them together but divide them between the sunflowers and spread them all over the construction. Lastly put the decorative beans very naturally on the base.

Design The strong base and the choice of colour and shape harmonise the whole bouquet. The circles give it a transparent feeling. The combination of colours, shape and flowers gives the bouquet a powerful impression in a modern way.
Technique The most used technique is binding. By connecting all the little circles, the construction gets a round shape. Because of the radial binding technique the construction holds the flowers on the right place.
Emotions This bouquet gives me an idea of a field full of sunflowers. It gives me a bright and happy summer feeling.

57

Autumn's gold

Designer
Per
Materials
Eremurus 'Cleopatra'
Nerine
Celosia
Phalaenopsis
Hypericum
Chilli peppers
Coloured wooden sticks
Mizuhiki wire
Plastic ribbon

Design A circle shaped radial bouquet with a wire structure that blends into the design. The idea here is to repeat the compact inflorescence of the Eremurus with smaller lines, berries and flowers, creating one light transparent design.

Technique Radial and wire structure are just as important to this design but at different stages of the work. Keep to the order described in the step by step instructions and work precise! The most important step is twisting the Mizuhiki wire. Work with straight pieces of wire, this makes it stronger!

Emotions The tranquillity and calm of autumn. The rich colours of the season glowing in the warm light of the sun, those last memories of summer.

1 To create this design of autumnal colours and gold use lots of smaller materials and lines that accentuate the strong but still transparent Eremurus. Clean all green from the flowers, to keep transparency as well as to create a warmer colour scheme.

2 Connect the Eremurus stems to each other using Japanese Mizuhiki wire, thin gold paper covered wire. Cut the wires in half and connect three stems with each wire. Twist the wire twice firmly around the stem and go on to the next, twist again and so on. Do this in an overlapping manner and on different heights in order to create good stability.

3 Keep the structure on the table, make a spiral and connect the last two stems. Cut all stems evenly and put the bouquet in a vase enabling us to decorate and protect the wire ends. Put Hypericums on the wire ends and dab the slightest dot of glue on each end first.

Autumn's gold

4 For more stability and decorative use, insert the coloured wooden sticks. Weave the shorter pieces through the Mizuhiki wire, going in all different directions. Place Chilli peppers on some of these for purely decorative use; no need to cover these ends!

5 To add more flowers take the bouquet out of the vase and untie it again. The structure is now so stable that it keeps together on its own. Work all flowers and grasses into the bouquet weaving them in between the wires and sticks, all into a spiral. Tie everything together using coloured plastic ribbon. Remember to keep it open and transparent.

La diva

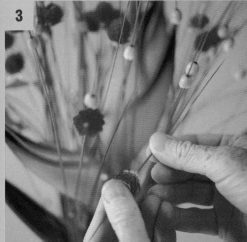

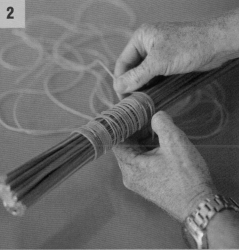

Designer
Per
Materials
Heliconia
Steel grass
Gloriosa rothschildiana
Hypericum
Gomphrena
18 gauge wire
Coloured wooden sticks
Plastic ribbons
Pins

1 Pierce Hypericums and Gomphrenas on 18 gauge wire. Remember to take off all the green parts on the flowers that do not dry beautifully.

2 Heliconia, Steel grass and coloured sticks plus our single Gloriosa are then put together in a parallel system and cut evenly at the bottom. Use colourful plastic ribbons for tying, they accentuate the almost plastic feel of the Heliconia. Make one wider binding place to level up the weight of the flower.

3 The pre-pierced Hypericums and Gomphrenas are then put on each single stem of Steel grass. Try to put them more or less on the same horizontal level.

4 Once the grass-stalks get berries on them they will fan out in all different directions! To prevent this and make one stricter shape, adjust them to the Heliconia using pins in matching colours. Pierce the pins through one or several grass-stalks into the stem of the Heliconia. Arrange the Steel grass in a crossing manner to avoid using too many pins.

5 Here you can see how the pins are worked into the grass and the Heliconia. Also notice how all colours and materials match each other. The main idea is: similarities instead of contrasts!

Design This parallel bouquet is made to show the character of the Heliconia. The lines accentuate its height and pride and every small detail focuses on this fantastic flower. Observe the colours, how they harmonise in similarities and not in contrasts. The colours of the Heliconia decide, it is a 'natural colour system'.
Technique The technique consists of parallel binding and the pinning of details. Follow the shape of the Heliconia in this bouquet. So, when working all lines together, remember to cross and almost weave the grasses together as well as pin them into the Heliconia.
Emotions Joyful, fun and kitschy! Rich personality that is expressed in the strongest of ways. Pins and plastic ribbons further emphasise the plastic almost artificial feel of the Heliconia.

Connected ellipses

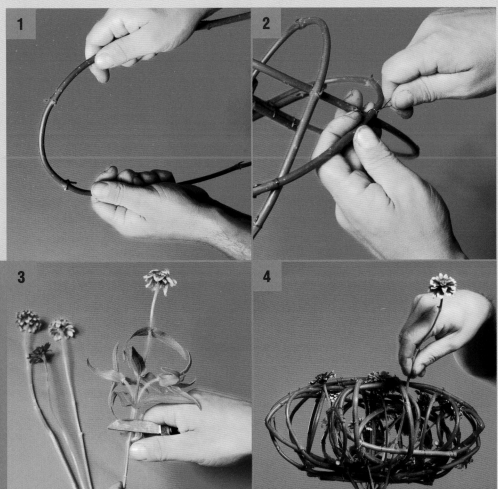

Designer
Max
Materials
Cosmos
Zinnia elegans
Cornus alba 'Siberica'
Red wire
Natural rough rope

Design This parallel arrangement is made of Cornus ellipses. These are connected without any symmetry, but with depths and heights. Seen from the top, it is a circle. The flowers are placed in different levels in the bouquet, without any foliage so that it keeps its transparency.
Technique The construction is decorative but also a technical help for putting flowers in their place at the intervals you want. Remember to add flowers first on the outside and then on the inside.
Emotions The final, transparent bouquet is sweet, clear with many different angles. It looks powerful, but also a bit dominant … And that with only three kinds of material. The colours of the deep dark Cosmos and the bright Zinnia make it a bit mystic too.

1 Bend the Cornus branches into ellipses, fastening the ends with red wire.

2 Attach the ellipses together in different angles, so that you get a round construction seen from above. Also make a handle from the Cornus. This will be the stem of the bouquet.

3 Take the flowers and remove all the leaves, to get smooth, bare stems.

4 Now arrange the flowers in different layers. The Cornus construction keeps them where you want. Don't use too many flowers to keep the transparency.

Connected
ellipses

5 Bunch the flowers together in a parallel bouquet, twist a cord around 5 cm of the stem and cut all the stems even.

Circling canes

Designer
Tomas
Materials
Anthurium
Sambucus
Bouquet frame
Iron wire
Canes
Black spray paint

Design This round bouquet has a flat design with a slightly conic shape. Its tiny top makes it more elegant and gives it more power. The weaving technique and the use of differently sized canes give the bouquet more movement.

Technique This radial bouquet owes its firmness to the woven construction. Use a bouquet frame to make a solid base. This arrangement requires a good weaving technique and two kinds of canes: solid and smaller ones. The weaving technique holds the flowers in the right position.

Emotions The spiral movement in the bouquet gives a fluent and good flowing feeling. The flowers act as natural ingredients in this movement: a natural harmony.

1 Use a bouquet frame as a steady base to weave on later. First spray-paint the frame black so that the iron of the base won't jar too much with the black canes. Put eight strong canes crosswise and vertically on the frame for support, making a conic shape.

2 Weave the canes through the iron frame. Begin with the thick and strong ones for the base and work from the bottom up to the middle. If the canes are too sturdy and keen to break, put them in water to make them more flexible. The first ten ones have to be tied onto the frame.

3 Now entwine the canes one by one till they form a firm construction. To make the shape more perfect, use the firmer canes first and then the smaller ones. Weave them through the thicker ones. Use the thinner ones at the top.

4 Put the flowers into the construction by squeezing them between the canes. Use the radial technique to make a wider arrangement without breaking the flowers. Start with the berries and divide them all over the bouquet. Use the flowers to give the bouquet some points of 'rest'.

71

Pierced Callas

Designer
Per
Materials
Zantedeschia 'Schwarzwalder'
Gomphrena globosa
Ixia
Phormium
Vuylstekeara Cambria
Mizuhiki wire
Bullion wire
Pins
Plastic ties

1 The main material for this piercing technique is Japanese Mizuhiki wire: thin, long, strong, paper covered wire in two metallic colours. But also needed are pins, plastic ties and bullion wire.

2 Cover the bottom 2 to 3 cm of the stems with the bullion wire. This way, the stems won't split and you get a nice colour contrast with the flower part.

3 Put the Callas down on the table surface in the shape you want and bind them together in a radial system. Make spaces in between the Callas by piercing the stems with wires. Do this crosswise to stabilise the design and to keep the flowers from pulling back to each other again.

4 Then cut all the wire ends into a fan shape. Pierce decorative materials such as Gomphrena on the wire ends. Also add other materials on the Calla stems using pins and ties.

Design The intention is to create a bouquet in a different, interesting shape, a shape that shows the Calla in all its beauty! The overall impression is light and almost fragile, but the structure itself is strong and stable. It is also a bouquet for a special occasion, considering all the pinned details of the fresh materials.
Technique The whole structure is based on the piercing technique. By piercing the stems of the Callas and doing this in a crossed system, you get good stability. Using thin Mizuhiki wire you cause as little damage as possible and do not harm the flowers or shorten their lifespan.
Emotions The idea was to show the beauty of the Callas and their stems, to get a stricter and cleaner expression, characteristic of the rigid and proud Calla.

Cornus in bloom

Designer
Tomas
Materials
Cosmos
Cornus
Rosa
Styrofoam ball
Iron wire
Bouquet frame
Black paint

1 Cut off the upper part of a styrofoam ball and use the biggest half. Cut branches of Cornus to similar pieces of ca. 8 cm.

2 Attach of strong iron wire to each Cornus twig. Add the bouquet frame into the foam with hot glue. The frame will hold the styrofoam and the flowers on the right place.

3 Paint the ball and the bouquet frame black (similar to the colour of the Cornus) and put the twigs one by one, next to each other into the styrofoam. If necessary, put a little bit of glue on the wire ends so they will hold better into the styrofoam.

4 First add rose branches. It is important to put them in a natural, hanging way. The next step is to finish the bouquet by adding the delicate Cosmos flowers. Once again the structure of the frame keeps the flowers in place.

Design This decorative bouquet is built around the branches. The Cornus pieces are protecting the flowers like a wall. Colour harmony is important here. Put the flowers also between the branches to create the idea that everything is natural.

Technique The main technique is preparing the little Cornus sticks and putting them into the styrofoam. The use of the bouquet frame holder makes it all more easy. The flowers are tied in a radial way.

Emotions The Cornus protects the delicate flowers. We used the strong, 'masculine' Cornus to protect the innocent, shy flowers. Each flower has its character, it is nice to play with this.

Clear fan bouquet

Designer
Max
Materials
Ornithogalum arabicum
Papaver somniferum
Scabiosa caucasica
Allium sphaerocephalon
Echinops ritro
Setaria italica
Aluminium wire
Plastic ties
Waterproof flower tape
Coloured bullion wire

Design This parallel design is made of a frame of coloured aluminium wire shaped in spirals, which gives the bouquet a great decorative value. Also, the bare stems made it more transparent, light and graceful.
Technique Make the spirals and the construction first. Push the flowers through the spirals so that they are fixed where you want them. Thanks to the tape they will stay put. Best is to use flowers with bare, flexible stems or flowers of which all greenery has been removed.
Emotions We created a powerful bouquet that is clear and strong, but also elegant. The parallel lines and the spirals bring in movement that makes it all very attractive and surprising. Also, the base makes it a very solid construction.

1 Cut aluminium wire into pieces of 50 to 75 cm. Make spirals of different sizes on both sides of the wire; it is important that they don't curve. You need ca. 30 pieces. Also make 30 pieces of 40 cm with spirals on only one end.

2 Intertwine the spirals one by one and fix them with two or more plastic ties. Cut away the redundant plastic from the ties.

3 Arrange the small spirals on the outside of the fan and put the bigger ones more near the middle. Stretch the wires with empty ends carefully to make a nice handle. These ends are gathered together and tied on two spots with some waterproof flower tape. This way, you get a powerful construction for your bouquet.

4 Spread the various flowers all over the construction and attach the flowers with the flower tape. Finish by covering the tape with bullion wire in the same colour.

Love!

Designer
Per
Materials
Dianthus
Lathyrus
Ixia
Gomphrena globosa
Cotinus coggygria
Aluminium wire
Spool wire
Pins

Design The commercial version of 'Circle of summer' (p. 43). The original way with wires gives us more options on decorating, but this is quicker and easier. The decorative flowers besides the carnations create shadow effects. This is not only a technique for carnations, all flowers with thicker stems or heads can be used.

Technique Adjust the gauge of wire to the quality of the carnations. This won't shorten their lifespan if you use good wire that is not too thick. Work as instructed and keep the stems on the table until the spiral is done.

Emotions Love! What else? The bouquet that definitely says more than words … It might be for Valentine's Day, a day of impulse. Or that most important one, the day you ask her to marry you. Put the box with the ring inside the heart and propose, she can not say no!

1 The structural material for this bouquet is aluminium wire. Strip all the leaves except the two top ones from the carnations. Take 1.5 m of wire, cut a sharp edge on it and pierce the flowers.

2 Pierce the carnations in the lower, thicker and sturdier part of the head so as not to split them. This is described in the circle shaped bouquet on p. 43, but is even more important here because the aluminium wire is thicker. Flatten the line on the table surface.

3 Once all carnations are on one line, connect the first and last at the pointy edge in one carnation and secure with spool wire. Make the spiral still on the table surface, tie it together and put in a vase. Then you make the heart shape first by simply bending the wire carefully not to break any carnations.

4 Then it is up to your own desire to decorate the bouquet. Tie in more flowers, more to one side making the heart a bit irregular. Also use pins to attach details onto the carnation heads. Finally cover the binding place with some spool wire in a matching colour.

A fan of fall

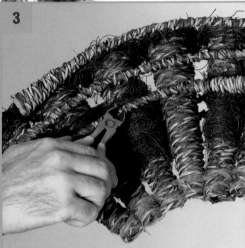

Designer
Tomas
Materials
Hydrangea
Dahlia
Rose-hips
Daucus carota dara
Panicum
Platanus
Pipettes
Iron wire
Natural rough rope

1 Use pipettes that are easily available. The texture has to be strong – most of the time they have a strong plastic centre – to make our fan design. The idea is to use those cones to support the flowers and to shape the bouquet.

2 Cut the ends off the pipettes. Now tie several short cones to each other in a radial way by using a piece of natural and rough rope. Tie the cones with iron wire for better fixation.

3 Use the ends of the cones to make the whole more solid. Put them in a nice way on the radial construction and tie them with iron wire. The decorative element is a nice extra aspect.

4 Fill the pipettes with flowers. Thanks to the pipette construction you get a radial bouquet. First put all the berries into the cones. Then add the bigger flowers like the Hydrangeas. Finish with the more delicate flowers. Finally stick some Plantain balls on it with glue. Fix the stems together with the same rough natural rope.

Design The radial bouquet of connected pipettes is a fan construction with a different design. The use of red and brown colours makes a good harmony.
Technique Binding the six pipettes together is the first important step. This will be the base of the bouquet. Make sure they are in one line. Put the flowers into the cones and complete the arrangement by binding the stems in a radial bunch.
Emotions The emotion here is one of autumn. It is like a 'fan of fall'; if we open it we can see fall in all its facets. We end the year in beauty.

Natural harvest bouquet

Designer
Max

Materials
Pear wood
Apple wood with apples
Malus 'Red Sentinel'
Viburnum opulus 'Compactum'
Aralia continentalis
Rosa with berries
Rubus fruticosus
Phytolacca
Thymus
Kiwi
Natural rough rope

Design This decorative, parallel bouquet is made of materials from the same habitat and season. We made a strong cylindrical shape with the Pear wood and filled it with the red, orange, green and black berries.

Technique Start by making the construction of Pear wood. Fill in with the berries, but don't fill it too much. Keep open spaces for the growing effect. It has to look natural. It is important to follow the step by step instructions.

Emotions The intention was to make a sturdy, strong harvest bouquet that suits the materials and the season. We worked in the natural way the materials asked for, so that it became a perfect harmony.

1 Select pieces of old Pear wood by their shape: they have to fit into a cylinder. Fix them together with spool wire. Keep one straight stem in the middle that will be used as the stem of the bouquet.

2 Then secure all heavy materials like Apple wood branches onto the frame using spool wire. Don't fill the middle of the bouquet too much.

Natural
harvest
bouquet

3 Add the materials from the top down to the bottom of the bouquet. Make it more transparent in the top and more full at the bottom. Also cluster groups of materials together – don't just mix everything.

4 Make a nice, cylindrical shape. Finish off with Thymus and cover the stem with a long stretch of cord.

In summer fields

Designer
Per
Materials
Triticum aestivum
Lathyrus
Rosa
Astrantia major
Cotinus coggygria
Limonium 'Emille'
20 gauge wire

1 Cut the wheat stalks above the last knot and insert wires into the stalks, all up into the top. Use a dimension of wire that matches the size of the stalks, 20 gauge for instance.

2 Put the wired stalks in water all the way up to the top for about 20 minutes. This softens the straws and makes them flexible.

3 Then make a construction by crossing the stalks at the middle and twisting them around each other. Start with two and add new ones, continuously crossing and twisting until you reach the shape you want.

4 Start at the centre and work your way out. Always add new stalks so that you create new long ends to build on further. Cut off any visible wire ends and make a handle from three stalks that you attach under the centre of the structure.

Design This decorative radial bouquet is built around a construction of wired wheat. This allows us to create a transparent expression. To enhance this even more, reduce all greens and foliage and work with a pink, grey-green colour spectrum.
Technique Start by making the construction. Then add flowers at the base as well as at the top, all in a radial system. Allow space between each of the materials.
Emotions The intention was to recreate the feeling of a summer field in full bloom. We enhanced that moving, light and transparent feeling by using a construction as a base and accents of pastel summer flowers.

Circles of scent

Designer
Max
Materials
Rosa 'Zaffiro'
Mentha tigra
Monarda
Allium sphearocephalum
Rosmarinus officinalis
Origanum
Thymus vulgaris
Salvia leaves

Design This decorative, radial bouquet is made out of very differently scented materials that give it an extra value. The classic, circular build-up gives all the flowers and other materials the attention they deserve.

Technique Clean all the flowers starting from the same height. This makes them more easy to work with and equalises each circle. Pay attention to the succession of materials. Look at structure and colour.

Emotions We put an extra emotion within this bouquet: the emotion of scent. It is an important one because we use it too less. Still, it can open new doors. Working with scents in a classical shape will remind us of the good old days.

Circles of scent

1 Clean all flowers starting from 10 cm below the heads and assort them by kind on the table. Then take them in a radial bundle in your hand.

2 Now add full circles of flowers. Each time, a circle of open material (Mentha) alternates with a circle of material that fills the openness again (Salvia leaves).

3 While making the layers, make sure that every circle differs in colour and structure. This makes them stronger.

4 Finish the bundle with corral fern, tie the stems together with a cord and cut them nicely.